Continuations
Douglas Barbour and Sheila E. Murphy

Continuations
Douglas Barbour and Sheila E. Murphy

The University of Alberta Press

WITHDRAWN

Published by

The University of Alberta Press
Ring House 2
Edmonton, Alberta, Canada T6G 2E1

Copyright © 2006 Douglas Barbour and Sheila E. Murphy

ISBN 10: 0–88864–463–9
ISBN 13: 0–888644–63–3

Library and Archives Canada Cataloguing in Publication

Barbour, Douglas, 1940-
    Continuations / Douglas Barbour and Sheila Murphy.

(Currents)
ISBN-13: 978-0-88864-463-3
ISBN-10: 0-88864-463-9

    I. Murphy, Sheila E., 1951- II. Title. III. Series:
Currents (Edmonton, Alta.)

PS8553.A76C654 2006   C811'.54
C2006-900222-3

A volume in Currents, *(cuRRents)* a Canadian literature series.
Jonathan Hart, series editor.

The University of Alberta Press is committed to protecting our natural environment. As part
of our efforts, this book is printed on Enviro Paper: it contains 100% post-consumer recycled
fibres and is acid- and chlorine-free.

The University of Alberta Press gratefully acknowledges the support received for its pub-
lishing program from The Canada Council for the Arts. The University of Alberta Press also
gratefully acknowledges the financial support of the Government of Canada through the
Book Publishing Industry Development Program (BPIDP) and from the Alberta Foundation
for the Arts for its publishing activities.

Canada Council   Conseil des Arts
for the Arts   du Canada   Canadä

For Sharon
and for friends in collaboration everywhere
D.B.

As always, with gratitude to Beverly Carver
S.E.M.

Acknowledgements

Thanks to Alethea Adair who first showed
interest in *Continuations* and took it to the
Press and pressed for its publication, then
found a superb reader and worked with
us to make the poem the best it could be.
We are also grateful for the editorial
suggestions of Roo Borson, which aimed
us in the right direction on a number of
fronts. Thanks to designer Marvin Harder
for his elegant treatment of our text, and
to Michael Luski for herding the project
through in such good time. It has been a
great pleasure to work with the University
of Alberta Press.

Thanks to the editors of the following: *Lynx*
(online), above/ground press, Housepress,
Backwoods Broadsides, *The Word Hoard* (UK),
Masthead (online), *poetics.ca* (online), *BlazeVOX*
(online), *Queen Street Quarterly* (Canada),
Rampike (Canada).

i.

> sturm und
> wrangling
> with that angel always
> staring
> back upon
> the piling ruin
>
> solo fires thicker
> than   or wider
> wings spread to
> raise the ante
> 'in front of' the sun
> what signs float in the empyrean
>
> foreground of stranded
> sun   sans
> seamed mild
> blue eggshell
> her name, Celeste
> over a wing afield
>
> afar   or falling
> to sea   med or black
> meld or block that light
> 'translucent' and so wide
> the notes hang still above
> waves washing ultramarine
>
> as if / as in a colour seamed
> young ring chipped small
> haze blue's entrancing
> migrant light
> in tones as wide
> intoned

informed
in foam as white
retreats   the night
hostile blueblack now
a single star's chipper gleam
sews a dark possibility

treats nacht as stoic
empt— ever to be glanced upon
entirely potent
in its absent
gleam as
buried (lance)

where / temperature / was
sketched into / frost cloth's
preclusionary warming
trance (meanwhile)
a qualitative light brushed
health's own sacrament

channelled that bright
20/20 breath's
balm   blame
not the sacral sight
white shapes the air
behind those disappearing legs

(entonces) migratory venture
while appearing (still)
the sense of sight repairs
what has been missed:
logs on the fire   now dwindling
shapes as strewn things ...

at once the migraine censure
disappears (at will)
sensual at night stares
at what shifting possibilities
the embers fading
slip into the mind

as voice desired   husk
levelled into surfaces
sans colour   smoke, though,
in a night way   taking
free places into custody
to know them only silently

stepping lightly through
or across such cancelled
sights and sounds   a single leaf
floating   stretches
time, the reach of moon
lighting paths across the river and

some silver posse lined
to locate in the fallow trim
a blessing   wherewithal   speech
chanced upon per
the directional endeavoring
across and in and through

a word of limitless
long wide blue environment /
a word tainted by
crust (alas) that blocks
kinesis in around through
these lines

expanding means of weighing
transportation, runes stand
still to temper fleeting lithe scapes
seamlessly, improved
by the domain
of their recovery

du main / 'the ayre' which weighed
and shooed away by
lifts above both runes
and ruins fleeing
above (across) a sown
(sewn) blue blazon

chemistry / in fact / flecks
Cheshire golden in the time passed
swiftly around sanctions
uncontrolled damage (dommâge)
until the till and many
boundaries retract (such blue)

as fades to black or ultra
marine marooned
or kept behind such walls as
raise the roof beams of solid
cloud to whirl the lift of
loss of globe's glissade

lobe's impasse equals drama
quelled, if touch is all there is
to changing trees with scribble
on embarking,
so the journey is
from far enough away

ii.

a soft cough
in the broken branches
her remains
remaindered count
coup against the falling
market

count for her her
syllables before she thinks them
say them (falling) once
to brave third
person singular,
whose watch may have been over

given or taken
over   and out of
the box bravely expedited
she will take that first step
into statement against all odds
or all hope going   gone

art chills still or leaps from
corner, magnifies a clipping
traces pairs of brackets and
their innards course-corrective
plenary rubbed frame
watched open

the snow blow
chill the catch at
cornered newsflash in
face fact
or read   then watch
political candles flicker (out

but inadvertently as miracles
occur, as streets lay open
feathered whole and smooth,
thus shapely when the falling
traces pass settled
traces unobtrusively from far

did that star intrude?
the unobserved remains
remains of art's other
laced with un or
disbelief and traced (tracked)
through vast desarts of   oh

craft found in
interstices vast, pearled,
colour that betrays
delinquent fire with/in
eye lacklusting after
ever aft

behind that small boat
mooning through the starscape
you'll find some /
thing thought there that
tells   tolls
what ends begin to

crux its way through
water / decibels / streetnoise
(if there is) tolls telltale
praxis in the wake
the waft of shelf
and sugar

coated   ghosts of
tales past and future
the narrative sailed beyond
the sunset sky's
fathering myth's
faltering misses

faithful to the hilt
of screen gem salted
though relaxed as if
(as if to say) retired
declaration independently
alert

to what purpose
might be said to be said
as the declared night
approaches   flocks
flaks filled the skies with
or the snowy hills

cease flowing toward what
sensed paint threatens
to have branched in flocks
to dampen wilt blue skies
defining the filled
sequel silence

'farre off' that translation
all belief seeks
sought   or a sough
through leaves turned
as 'we' turn to trace
quests across white space

listing, listening, fibers few
enough, ingratiated to relaxed
toned mode in surface sweet
to venerate what whistling
soffits seethe to gather
weeds and choice results

how folded   where woven
in the fold   starred
standing fields offered choices
even just earth hold
sky in her embrace
in a different lower room

even instants likely have been
softened when away with
this fueled simmering
chastisement of the body
sweetly / held / as young
thinning its way to our fruition

which will come
out from under softening
earth house hold held no longer
back ('i' speak from
the cold north; 'i' say 'snow'
hard body birthing only beneath future suns

pralined against imagination verily
as thickets warm themselves
apart from houses north of
birth tones / rafters / glib recourse
to have intended the beneathment
of a sugar thumbed to wait list status (this)

iii.

tainted or tanned shadow
twists and then holds hard
arrowed out but cut casually
down the long line of lighter
green between trees
up and over toward the faraway

elapsed as startling white
wings chaperone the dreams
they cauterize, again light
green, trees trace their losses
in a distance close cut, tresses
replenish origins, fill skies

eclipsed or shadowed face
hiding eyes refuse to reflect
branches break the light
to small parcels of
bright colour lasering
darkness' heat death dying out

in circles, chemistry infracts
the leisure swathes of symmetry
among the cogs draped with enactment
held in memory's less
sharp blades
pressing temperatures

does memory stay frozen or
burn up when the engine's
sly vanes turn and turn
thrown gears gut imagery
as the grind grows toward
mirrored sound refracted

toned, impacted, lunging toward
what will abide / questions
simmer verblessly, verbena
likely chides the mirror
full of imagery in sound
on continents always hinged

a long time ago
then dis-jointed the flow
of time compacted seas
while all the mountains   leas
left all behind / who cares
what forests rocks and flowers tears

high places rearrange reality
via arbitrary views made local,
in a logical perspective,
trees are gladed in a surplus pasture
arranged, perceived
exclusively from afar

who stands alone there
in such local shade
finds vision unmade for
communal 'needs' so unconjoined
to home place felt now as
fall of fractalled possibility

is it just tethering, the clearly
seen shade muting vivid
sparks apart from blue
that signals solo act,
distinct from particled arrangements
once agreed upon

and who would speak
to such conjunction of each
piqued stand above Darien
upon each separate point
of order corralled
to discussion dissevered

plunked, even, where and when
and if the seen is jointed
so another thatch is whimsical
at last, discretionary planks
make room for livening
the act of point on point

'sunday in the park' while george
painted (out) the land's scape
escaping land into oil's whims
wanting or waiting upon
vision's vindication
to play toward what's seen as scene

as veering toward a vast
en-scène the Seine extravagantly passes
flecks of the imagination sprawling
to amass ingredients perceived as possible
forming a larger thing
of something small

through years as well as tears
in the fabric of what vast canvas
delicate flicker of light
across fluid movement of
the real realized now as already
lost and gone, imagination's neglected reach

frost cloth's own sequence
of protecting what prepares,
the limitation on a being
to provide quench, light,
structure, even years
of posture for another

how light a melting fall
across flame's feeble wash
floats chiaroscuro's contra
how brightly oil's pall
denotes punk beauty
as a young saint sin(g)s a loud

outside / the plan's / diminuendo
pitch gone stuck with world
entangled in worlds stolen
by discomfiture in speech,
faith, weeds, infinite
icicles that last almost as land

crisscrossed by a reaching out
through forest's dark to light
a flame a faith
in future's household / now's
holdings worth all spirit's
investment or investiture, taken

quipped, seeded, scorched,
or turreted, the holdings
quease away from us until
we barely notice we have left off
faith and dried our hands
and practiced living on a wage

to pray for prey on
in that hooped cathedral
of digits moving so fast
faith can't keep up to
fingers crossed and crossing
its built heaven's scoreboard

catching glimpses
of young truth
that feather just away from
crossing fields that highlight
movement crossed and crossing
shaped like worship

iv.

out toward the fading light
of day gone, star fallen's
feather drift's a fire inscribed imploded
but beyond bibliograph
spoken's dream said outward
flare offers freedom as gift

practice, fever, strongarm, fate,
the lavish choices drift from fire
the salsa has imploded
here goes speaking on a bet,
a flare, a roster or a feeble
rose to centre what we favour

fate fêted felt as always
already done beforehand's
not what we bargained for
forests fall unheard there
as the river fills
with land thrown out to sea

with sea itself tossing
the lighted trinkets smothered
by momentum tainted near
the frost of havens heard
as land below
the weeds of a priori

choice? a sleight of
hand or brand name
the weight of it
buckles iron and oil
as the slick sticks
life to rock and won't let go

or are whisked off into
dowries, diaries, dailies,
fated to have happened,
meaning clipped out of a larger
text and held as though
lui-même, in place, apace

'a step away from' us
heading always out beyond
the next turn in the narrative
nation's that or pro
gress' gram gaining
speed   refusing onus

a few of these weigh in,
the onus on us
splintering toward
shared narrativity,
this happened that then
is this progress

the grain of it
turned again away from
chopped   slashed
'a field of' untold stories
left behind under carbon glare
not a glance for the fallen

paced / stirred / woven
over time the tales become
familiar, while the faculty of surprise,
muted, grows into parsnips
perfectly inedible with history
to claim or point to-ward

protection from
the garbage piling up behind
discarded rinds unseen un
eaten while human retelling
retooling for the future beyond
the tales tolled for getting and spent

laden with windsock misadventure,
pray to preach a mid-day cure
for sadness evidenced in tools
torn from the tales we won't repeat,
'one integer or two?' canards
compete with selves finding the surface

tools or fools for
the hammers of politesse
used up up
ended from cargo bays
rusted bones in salt
water wait without hope

is there a virtue to match
salt, the gatherings, a pungent
fusion of collective noun and
individual ingredients, each
each each draws out
of one the many

re: turns the twists of
DNA refute denial
of collective and
we begin like   how
now discover connective
song sung into emptiness

to ride around it   levered
see how over water
new quests iterate evasion toward
the press repealed concisely
into our natural falling away
let loss show falsefronts reverting

plentifully to the left as
hefted into consciousness concisely
lolling where the front is true
reversion pressed against evasive
nature in a tuned fun glow
to beach the rail of quest

balls float in the dark blue
air across the sand indented
by 'flying feet' and arms
outstretched in a kind of
joy joined to the frugal
fragmentation of waveforms perceived

postponed equals deleted delta
'are you there yet are we whole'
the sand on which outstretched
we like with joy's own opposite
frugality in frag
formed waves of the favoured blue

moving slowly from sea
to beach to sift through
eyes as clouding over
crowding ever closer to
subject activity arms raised
to the shining ball hung there in suspense

after effects loosen glare
of a supposed sky, quiet,
ever shining guesses
raised to the reach
of a suspended motion
beached where eyes sift seasons

v.

held there in the mind
moving with sun through
predictable motions   as
a century's crash and rush
of foam the litter of later days
floats flags in the cooling air

swollen pollen flies up and over
grasses greening in bright sun
belled bees caught tomorrow then
fractalling outwards
to eventual liquid white as
the paddocks unpedlocked tasted

fresh, spliced, foraged, all the things
we know in pieces,
even hue's refraction
under a bright sun
spinning whole host bees in plenty
yards and sakes 'til liquefied

years sucked up tally
a carted lore lent
heavy presence centred
where gathered and transformed
to wise concentrate licked
a spoonful at a time

in transit, synthesized nineteen
seventy-eight Metheny with
mockingbird, only a window
in between one and another
fact in concentrated hearing
where the rigours are relaxed

glass between or gloss
that open space and empty
of her presence unheard
was it ten years after
or earlier they spoke out
through technology deferred

saved in the way events are
held and changed, even
surprised into the recognition
of exactness as unfit
for rendering what was
recorded as imagined

nice and accurate
what she said there
out of the box where
event itself was held
in suspense pending
desire's desperate predictions

what happened next was, and what
won't occur, become the same
influx until suspense binds
desperation to objective case
fraught with accurate desire
expended on case-closed intervention

to construct a law against desire
might clear desire's rep
a rap sheet contra servicing
an adult obsession
what hurts is what hurts so
polis says 'it hurts me too'

commandments spawn likely ingenuity
pronouncing antithetical disjunction
everywhere and from each spigot
of new grace indented
things to have obsessed on
as adults might do when hurt

when were they hurt
those obsessive ones coming
to the same conclusion again
and again disjunctive in fear
and trembling on the verge of
breaking from commands meant

comatose commands tweak live
young, old guilts very plural
in obsession, coming to the same
fear lined with vibrati chock
flavored with verge and nearly
broken in anticipation of the hurt

and can't take it this time
again yet do each time
twisted further into use
less repetition spoken
on the couch again   again
they wait for the shock of

only flowers, less shrill
than thought   previous things
furtively perhaps press in
on nerves and foster
longing for the couch again
st ore/d filaments   of what

mouth opens to silent snow
falling so gently   beyond
transparence   transference
discretion   each frozen flower
blossoming above a hand
held nervous out and opening

to another likely or
unlikely flower in states
of the imagination (gently)
writhing past be
yond the non
existent

chores of reformation climb
thought, detritus grows
to be the stepping
strictures, conveys
its being day's work,
even silent art

even silent heart out
going to the mulch there
colours run and the black
of coal dust whet the edge of
each sure stroke
struck out for construct's end

to make is to exceed
currency, dramatic contrasts
lift the mulch to colourdust
as edges stroked to friction
ending most simplicity
with silence

unspeak excess by borrowing
against time's own
sweet temptation
to colours delved from eyes'
own(ed) depth of
pestled parturient

nestled small ones to be
sweet with eye fresh
time to waste or earn
more time to colour
in a season's measured
kind of tithing

vi.

tossing colour out
or in   to the scratched
surface of things   of
paper canvas catching
light / dark / all
wafted inbetweens

a visible thought's
mobility exempt from surface
the eye transcends repellent
crossing into new reach
captured on canvas, stasis
lacking blood, desire

yields an ever-changing
song or poem the sliding
white ink of instability
s crunch and roll
about time about
the stretch of it out to horizon's long line

with no origination fee,
heap big blasphemy, or slopes
right where the motion ought to be,
there we are, taming, bridling,
casting shadows with the thickness
of an answer to a prayer

intuited   felt in the fingers
hoping   hopping across
the solid sheet taking eyes'
thought drummed in
to lines leaned into free
hand   inked in to it

where music / play / strays,
is fixity at one
specific moment thrummed-in
lines spawn sweetness
inked in recollective
page on page of speaking

singing all those black
dancing dots in unison
lift up above the page
to lips opening a choir
s held tone   note after
note rising toward the sky

night-gathered tones
retreat into the tall cloak
covering light's thin,
young dance redeemed
by random song
transcending innocence

among the stars or planets
only in their planes   great
circles of light dance trans
mogrified to music
s tonal gold gleaming
against history's dark

appendages all melded into
thrumming chores that bend
alignment to a new refraction
timed / toned / up
lifted toward historically
formed gravity

holding down each
diurnal moment of attention
to   to do   to turn
the hand to   bring on the light
and look to windward   catch
the new breeze braving unto

how awareness used to be,
compared to how awareness is,
less hand than thought,
less heart than usually felt,
all need for bravery one does not
perfectly acknowledge anymore

body's loss
soul sad at how
all five precision instruments
slowly rust yet push
the figure of outward
outward still despite

quiet, infinite-seeming
coolness with only weather
to distract or soothe,
the instruments receding into
placement where their recollection
seems inaccurate as precision

readings   what possibilities
open through the glass to
LEDs or leads to follow
there's a line there   drawn
face faxed   fixed in rictus
from sterile environments gone

placid or violent or estranged
and always followed as though
lines were drawn where we had
fixed environments beneath
a pixilated qualmed sterility
gone to drawings in their place

in depth   indebted
to a sharp outline of
fuselied bodies caught
against the shadowed walls of
high dungeon   backlit
by fear brackets breaking

or external voicelets hunching
in audition to acquire
caught sentences aligned
and misaligned at once
the way a shadow sallies
in receding light

and who listens anyway
in the huge auditorium
darkness empty or full
do they   putative   hear
a complex music or the
shattered sense of syntax surprised

and even further into dis
connection, do they veer
back to intended selves,
or is the fall more sharply carved,
so a dividing line, once crossed,
becomes the defining moment

vii.

back and forth through
the unseen portals of intent
self selflessly sheds self
definition this time this
place cited in inscription's
cut and thrust read clearly

daily as repaired on the off
chance of being defined at last,
portals enlarge their destination,
each time / place thrusts
open into what remains
the permanent unseen

where each one has to go
through   and into   the vast
interior regions   opening
beyond expectations an
other I   frère   semblable
sees what you cannot say

that monking whit of sub vocal
prayer eventually saves both
conscious and unconscious
detainees in life, this
joins each expectation
to a moment of the other

in silent openings
dew ghosts against
leaves flow and ripple
above dawn glow up
standing there   listen
what moves outside

is inherently here
standing as above, so
( ) and flow to have been
listened to still
leaves as ghosts as silent
openings, what moves outside

moves back and through new
portals to the enlarging
inner worlds of ( )
irising beyond the reach
laid out in scattered light
flowing toward the falling moon

across those eons   suns
sail too   galaxies
dying   dying   centuries of
light lost   come to write
across what pages of night
unread   the sentence due

an audience / the looking on
indelibly for one pure
evident moment / relaxing toward
the final breath become
these centuries / viable
as galaxies / constructs

those arches overhead
stoned knowledge glow
as ink sheds light to shadow
forth exhalation's mist
finally evident the moment
re/turns a mirrored lack

of firsting / held, then
shed to light toned shadow
forth as evident
this moment arching
overhead turns
being mirrored

as circling it proffers bright
as penciled shadowing
suggests outlines out
of light toned down
under brush precisely catch
(cached) re flecks of fall

swept into outlines once
thought hewn, toned edges
mute the early light
that separates flecks
from wholeness fallen into
cache that teaches replication

mechanical?   or only thought
s to be there found
as cutting   edging   as there
now   in the midst of
chips strewn   the glare
illuminates the hidden

most thing s illumine thought
if the mechanical switches
are flicked on the hidden
thought s reply to midst
that amplify the local
anesthesia normed to match the harm

caught on the wing thought
s on the wind blowing back
through history's long
midden moiled high
archive of bone bane
lit by stormflash fittingly

precepts gleam due
left with history to bother
being the detritus false
and back known archive
in the fitting place
of keeping books and smudges

finger prints dirty news
flash five times blissed
outside history's box
of billets-doux duct
taped to technology's
dance across papers scat

sung purple-passaged
as the rest that follows,
jots of history's
boxtop opening to dance
flashed across the screen
that enters and remains

blank for the time
being there and shadowing
through   the fall the wings
swept backwards from
the muddle world midden
piled high to dance across

quaffed rinse lifting
middle things aglance with
shadow after fall from
time and various swept
flight accretes to islands
various and stunning

viii.

shunning variety's pebbles
flung   lost and / or found
occlusion   afloat triangled
shadows of plantations sufferance
suffices for a martial music
darkens and stuffs dance away

to sway and say the curfew
blanks out of some surfaces
split from centres,   all
plantations at angles
dark in part and being
found in places pebbling

in the rush and sway of
surf rolled across ribbed
beaches   rubbed ratcheted
riveted   how workers wait
beneath pith shades
staring around angles captured

metropolised   and hammered by
red eye in the sky
straining beneath obverse
observation everywhere
the they or we lost to
solitary refinement

where reason 'sects its turncoat
heart and chance devours
the feeling world hoped for
then slipped back into the fill dirt
of a measured shadow
palling corners in defection

get out, self, now, if you can
says heart   and chancing the door
ways find themselves open
but to where   harsh
lights shadow each path
to freedom is it or just escape

openings have shadows near
the heart's uneven
pathways   leading to warm
chance reversing some
recidivist dimensions, apart from
a small effort blue

wings or gills   the blue calls
for   forgotten   or falls
into the prisonhouse again
dive off the wall and
sink or swim eternal return
of daylight dimmed fathomed

undulation   flux   the willing
trespass of routine left off
return to walls and fences
psyche tells are permanent regard
less and less lightworthy
as dimness grows to the default

fingers make possible   but
tongued? the open door
or mouth   policy   the way
'we' seem to have a problem
of communication here
and there stuck inside of a song

a catch   all
consuming every mismatch
likely or not communion
splinters just shy of accomplishment
doors wide open smaller
and invisible doors stuck

to tear something
slipping in   slipping out
and move toward or away from
the tabula razed   the cup
held high   and somewhere
a light   blinding the eye

excursions partially recuperate
from exhausting routine,
and the reverse erasure
gleaming in past tense
slips from grasp
away from the probable intrusion

crisscrossing corridors
cut through the pile up
flashing lights make no sense
of carnage then who sings
to sign the loss of light
under all that dark cover-up

inferred, as realization
comes to be the same as
sur/faces progressively appear
from scraping what was last
made plain only
to be re/placed by the immediate

subject/ed alterity fied
and fried there, scrapings
of letters drifting to the floor
ed by every new turn of
phasing out the old making
way for pro aggression

a pulse is caught
pounding as prelude
to the old / making
a floor recalled
to status letters
transformed into thought

underfoot it shakes a shambles
as grooving into some new
beat beaten drum call
to dance beyond thought
thought beyond hierarchy
s call and response

a wafer thin drum tone
begins, then dance in flux
becomes scale model of desire,
the motive of percussion,
without event to stimulate
incessant seasons

modal of desire sharpened
against the rough beat
beat beaten floor bounce
bacchanal / backchannel
converse of shook foil
feel the shiver of skin beat

the slender drift of swan across
thin water passes gravity
toward rhythm shaken
from sleep's desire, glimmer
of crushed reflection
linking floor to tops of trees

ix.

a thin blue line hinged   to
the body caught
timed drowned   left
smugglish beautifully arraigned
/ detained / by the be
reft grounds taunted midrange

midrage   resistance rises
screamed   basso profundo
as bodies slowmotion   topple
a horizon line   list last
wave of   woof and weft
strung out musculature   sheered

backhand across the wash of strings
goes fleece of music, basting
cross-current of manifest domino
effect of frame within which
pleated atmosphere accepts
trance lightning change liaising

eclectic sonnet firearme
plushes strummed sin
indigo through
stirrup hexed in isles
extinguished lumps taken
in colour scored beyond within some same

banner shot silk streaming
windblown on the run or
chasing through all eight lines
then leap into dark
wonder   the smaller maze
colourbled   rivering

as riveting as cool   as still
reach to
ward blues-ed float crystal
in the meant fling jasmine
plied with wrought learned
notes with fingers   to / from aire

rendered transparent toward horizon
bloodcloud hanging fire
and the aquamarine floated trans
lucent lightfilled   fallen
no longer caught in the as
cendant   cinders now   percussing

parallel / equals / at peace
blooded and full / yet still
the lucent, lifted gleam of cinders
drive the coming night
as afternoon is pasture
caught in habits of trans/forming

habitude there a way off
on slung slopes beneath
green overhang   beneath high
peaks the reach of it
how seen from a deep chasm at noon
stars gleam stutter transparency

are we pure yet / doused with
lime-high peaks of fields still
focusing deliberation chasmically
on wakeful breast
beat before mourning
places from which reach attests

that things simple find exception
the exceptional gels into
simplicity, sub
speech, near
hearted, the intrinsic shards
reflect wholeness perhaps obscured

and moving into mist   under
shadow shift   dissipate   dis
appeared there   electric
air culled and called to
as singular   unified
and caught on the wing

still-pictured rasp of natural
flight appears as firm romaine
leaves tense and hold their liquid
in and through veins
lacing the unguarded workings
of an opposite disturbance

in candescence   in
rows   re
frigerated   and the way
light catches in each drop
greened   groined   be
leaved   greaved   opening

plankton stretched to mean
continuance perhaps / whose
magi number magical entrenched extraction
first caught light dropped from
pinned senses / fielded
sight to weigh / in rows

if ocean stretched out to receive
what   and   where faltered
filtered only   filigreed   shadows
moon/ worshipped/ whipped
typhoon crossing rows of
careful constructions tossed aside

trace the micro cord / to
find to (pause / pause)
locate worshipped stars
tucked under chaparral or mood
thus generously reverse(d)
instruction as construction casual or obvious

take two   too
much of the sound rises as waves
roil in white rush of
boarded   up to long lines of
mountain pointed to stars
stared at   believed in as

mesh inviting long maturity's
risen soil   a fine worn
mountain gravity set against
imagined waves   constructed
from belief   seen
white against what else

yet the flat of it the sheer
refusal of depth   the lines
how grave the greaves of pen
and ink   imaged toward
shared hope   the reach of
moon's grasp to take up

abstinence as sub
stance / perhaps one line
at a time   ink might mean
hope traced around planetary
fluctuations grasped if only
for the moment then released

as   ex   in
spires of notes raised
waterflecks flicked as
by a giant hand   so
delicate   traces
left leave just a thin dark line

x.

as taken thereon   as
gone into the world
of light substantiated into
voice / chanced / vibrating ground
absent to feathering (a) world
now conceived free   venturing

abstraction turned becomes
the actual, a sheaf of leaves,
the words there, needed patience
for discerning length and width
of strokes to be in motion
if / then left recalled

how 'we' called
culled from swept into
what's there   thought
less of   under mind
but not lost in bold
strokes   the the there

one take taken / bold strokes
minded mindful culling from / toward
mantra cooling ferment
of idée fixe
better all the time / the same /
thought there

host not lost not
gone from mind caught
catching now in tangled muchness
felt in every body motive
action there   mantraed
mandala   worlding

as the spring bird feeds
the autumn bird / a tangled winter
motive secular in action
equals the occasion
to relax upon / caught
host chancing benediction

let be the swash of
colour   let be
its moment   bird
in bush flash   tone
tangles   trompe
l'oeil   brushed stroked

one is smitten by
the beauty of mistakes
their unintended grace,
their swift resilience,
their resemblance to intention
shifted by a truer mind

no one knows   none
will say   or should
they will get it wrong
take laughter love take
hold 'error' its resilience
the grace of   gone now again

a perfected accident occurs
then disappears into
pale recollection initially unloved,
then learned into
a sharper, unplanned
form of exactness

precision of the curve
leaned into   how all is
tack and swerve   how
speed counts increasingly
if perfection sought piles up
the unnatural behind the beating wings

motion trills from set point
to hovering amid broad blue
on the off-chance migratory birds
confine themselves to gravity
what is shown in taut binoculars
evolves into a truth

and sings it out
rages even   as truth some
times will do   busted
chords   the bent note bending
time   telling tolls its own
farflung   wavelength   floated on

grasp, curved thought, electrodes
stirring with awareness,
notably when shared, the observed
changes the observer,
notes trim time to present
wave, achieving range

in   or through   star
grazing   dark
matters here   dark calls
from far and farther
sudden surge in black
holed beneath stone beneath notice

hovering across all things
mentioned, muted, strained into
invisibility on a scale ranging from
unnoticed to potent, focused attention
on any moment certain as a flower
with shelf life barely blue

slippery as the brush lifted
from bare canvas   as Monte
Ste-Victoire lifts
across not off the surface
tension of the eye
s knowledge of blue bluing further

toward levitesse, a gesture
that detaches surface from another
surface tension as immediately
colour pierces echoes of itself
further into slippage
as a brush resounds with what the eye

lies listening to the brush of
skins   the swish of rhythm
swirls colours homing and blue
tones surface as a note
bends narration   as depth
disappears   there   on top of

places to look down and across
toward expanse of clarity,
the illusion
of scarcity feigns erasure
of the rhythmic presence
told in tandem with existence

always the double voice
the double vision   side
by side on the clifftop
asked to choose why
do so   don't divide
take and   take all   take off

xi.

the everything available
occurs not for the asking
division's infinitely unnatural
but for growth upon the edge
of cliffs where scenes never are
so beautiful as to be taken

and setting sail subjects
the blue below to deeper ruts
running through a safety sought
elsewhere   a place there
blessed if token
taken away from minds made up

breath guides, the mind elides
a past too dark
to leverage rhetoric
too richly dressed and
dight as words step out
fitfully across the dark

a theorem fights off plain
text / irreality slows
fated motion to small spores
of chiding, once and twice
around the fitted block
beyond lost sway of words dis-membered

and floating round that corner
ed bricked and battened down
they'll find what hard ground
to child in   /   children
fall too   into muddy dreaming
textured to a hope beyond

the trappings of pragmatic ought
where whims are fried to honour
gravity's hard finitude,
dark brick charred with their resistance
and the outcomes of a walling off,
few things found down among repeated texture

where finally repetition falters
feeling toward pragma
dogma done in
cracked dome density im
plosive   posed as
a harsher question coughed out

what I thought
I heard,
a gust of swollen disavowal,
crumbs, the heart berated,
and the head, all of what
I always felt was there

and ran after
into dark wind through
trees roughed and tossed
heads in air / thoughts
thrown everywhichway
heard?   but listening?

motion fails to help
but motion is ubiquitous
mid-air solutions occupy
the head thrown into
rough toss of the heart
unheard till last

floated   like a loan
a cry from the heart
the drums of   the song of
the flight interrupted by
heedless / headless
the refuse of thought

discards given glow
smudge other thought
drums always underneath
thrum their way across non-song's
looming gravity continually
imparting the attention given interruption

drums of? drumming thought
out? away from the clear
into the smoke smudge growing
against any song's sure
hold on to skyblue sunburst
what falls from in darkness

is another stripe of song
or sun or cloud, percussive
and continuing less sure than
clarity and drums, what falls
into place is breathed
inimitably against the growing

march / i'd rather walk there
through a wood not
laid out squarely but meandered
strips of light and shade jangle
swung there on the off
beat jazzed cymbalic swing

and equally I'd lie still
listening to the shade be
dreamed from wood jazzed
slowly by little wind
only a scent of that
entire and with unstrained

heartfelt leaves drum
in the shadowed roots
held in there / the mind's
own clearing
of airs heard and sniffed
how smoke and dust disappear

and how they remain
stripped of their colour
textured in unclear pathways
leaving rooms and being rooms
held still or simply
felt as states of mind untraced

to turn back and follow
leaves stressed striations
swished silent or kicked into
out of which door
way of text your close read /
clearing a path unpuddled

xii.

there recedes a dry tone
to the path / door / text /
stressed fallow, so striations show /
a close read of the woman's television face
from over there / veiled, aged ten years
in just more than a month

lines in / lines from
the face faceted onscreen
a newly born text
ploughed and bombed fizz
ure made less now
hidden by a veil of words

born centuries from next
door ploughed still sizzling
beneath breastplate where
a veil shadows newborn
spate of feeling crimped
into a text hidden in lines

lined up then (and now
a crowded street a field
a text you're veiled in
screaming   torn from
what unempathic (emphatic)
valley thighboned / and clubbed thus

empty in an aftermath
of fractions   veiled spirits
screaming   empathy soaked in
blood bones lined
crossed in any field
known from below

to look up to and see
still and ever devastates
as veils form on body
after body felled
'if a tree' comes crashing down
if blood flows from a stone

the measuring / the measured
crash / the after-forms /
the blood in / felled tree /
spokes on the imagined /
vehicle to change / to have alleviated /
time twisted then veiled on / and to see

into the dark / there
where a single individual
small fire glows / embers /
and dies / and counts somehow
more to those who were lit
by that light / gone into

purer space considered from this
distance those beside remain
immune to what light kindled,
kindles still, one being
released at last from individuality
into a clearer peace

ashes already thrown upwards
smoke floats across the sound
of what's left in water falling
sunkindled sparkle
ing as one once did
to keep on toward that

pace of smoke tracing
water left in toward
the floats kin to
across tone keeping
toward already upwards
that sound ashen after

all fall down   or gone
into the lightest finger
ed note floated out from
over with /   single
and suddenly tripleted
chords knotted   as tightly

sunned where pace retrieves
a loosened cleave of whole
tones / three / over the light
from / down chords
scented with taut
ever aft

and trailing whispers
waves or weaves of
one element in an other
curved over and under
or carved / carried
years forward as felt there

being remote along the trailing
curvature   a blessing in
some sky   an element of carriage
years against the woven
underlight where forwarding
are wisps of felt waves in succession

smoothed   a handsign graced
by touch taken across
dunes, waves, the turn
of hip, or hair swept
up and across   to shift
memoried motion forward and up

motion outside self is often
thought the self /
the dunes / waves go with
wind / the turn of
what occurred before
then swept across

and turn of head / of mind
happens even as thought
strides to catch up   hurrying
in awkward slipsteps
through as across sand
swept up by trailing winds

flurry brings tangle
to the stride / nothing catches
up with hurrying /
in young tremblage
there is awkward quiet
happening across / found paths

for such a specific
desired one wan
and wandering / caught
up in clouded floating
over / lost now in
the shifting city's streets

principle discarded
leaves one wan / clouds cloth
as slow / shift migratory
deadlines seeping
from the lure of dis
personified desire

black hoods a bleakness
travelling beyond horizon
s treeline teethed to
catch last light / measure
mends borders crossed
by ligatures of light

joining's either accidental
or distended / crossing uneasily
defines that there are sides
measured or unmeasured
teething eventually breaks
through lines of trees to light

nothing perfectly
becomes / an accident until /
craft segregates the markings
that have whitened / loss
coursing / through foster
placement / randomly sustained

all those lost ones let go
whereof   wherever
accident allows / a gape
of love / a clutching of
the mother / the lines
owed to the paper placing there

the gap / a glove / would touch /
the *is* written on cellophane /
a random mother matched to
a lost child / lines drawn
placed to accidental
session after session / held in time

then moving out / and in
to systems transparent   and incised
with being (t)here
where mother and child (re)unions
sung below the mid / rash call
of leader / ship of the line

tines leave their tuning
a transparent shade etched
onto ritual, the clash
of wills eventually finds
parallel parades calling
for motion, being the motion

and moving on to tunes
glory has forgotten
if lost to life not lost
to memory / and not yet
offered up through the trans
plinth a ply of surface tension

placing place where life is
tuned to be the surface
over other surfaces until
the outermost layers begin
to touch and let go
tension after tension

traction after traction
at: (coherence) to
gather all remembering
moments scattered across
surfaces scraped and scratched
in script 'i' only hazarded

by way of ruse, repairs,
recall, the littered safety
patching script where it is
read to have cohered
in all the torque made
blest in moments

blast in moments airy
fix on illusive image
caught amid the scatter
slid and safe / tie the
twist and torque the weight of
writ / how it deceives (re)

maps well lit dis
close histoire or equally
the present tense
a scatterplot of ocean dust,
a ruse, plaits evidenced
by torque that weighs illusion

turns through cross
roads marked and sung
in note bent so / sew
some past story into
knots of territory
tensed toward inscription

that channelled blithering
preceding territory
when song inscribed its story
on the turned stones
equaling the tiny knots
intoning history

to forget as soon as knot
ted notes die / as death
become the territory claimed
tory terror's claim of
potency powered by
a repetitive tying (up)

concentration opposes / thereby
masks surprise
by claiming potent
f/right descending in
to repetons that bleat
too soon what will not be / forgotten

spread out as seen on screens
large and small glimmering
(scentless) a series / a thick
package of transparencies
camp over camp / the newly
dying cry havoc repeated and lost

fragrance recalls the inner
patchwork of a layered pulse
newly contiguous / screen
packages reply chanted
repeatedly until
the dying size still / flickers

screen within screen within screen
turns the night green and greener
fliff fliff the wings of night
flash / kneel with the morning
s call / walk out to finally
face the sun / is there food?

I want to gather something
white as silence is
presumed, I want to kneel
upon an afternoon's resiliency
night's own earned green
onscreen as wide as sentences resumed

and open to the clear
interpret via all roads lead
from / why is to the call?
I'd sit within that silence
reading all its changes
hearing those sweeter melodies

inclusive of harmonious clarity
the roads one reaches via
silence / within which changes
have interpreted the strand
of song / heard from the sweetness
leading to a reading of the call

xiv.

if 'I' am listening as i read it so
it calls beyond the me
an archaic possibility / a choir
ring: or round the pole of
overlapping counterpoint
bodying into the hurled heard

where tinctures wrest the clarity
by spoon from one full
glass of water / heard as counter-
point to speech or choir /
a body being simple
proximate to complexity

slips of colour flow down
ward through the clear
a twist of light / of sound
less song still wafting
waiting / wanting body
s clasp complex beyond

received nest, chapter, verse
pertains to certain
meaning possible, health eventually
grows a child, leads further
to a healing that appears
some new root

of temperate response, down-timing
slow depth when the pause means
waiting times, and children
taking turns with weather, tapestry
enlarges colour strewn
across the snow

lit up   the throw of
colour signs the slowing
down into a moment stretched
as childhood stays there
then / as a play of
light into the frozen eye

her picture in a year when she
seemed beautiful, even sounded
from the page the voice of
a deserved stretched focus,
placed beside the current look of years
the eye eventually releases

time to flow / how beauty
only seems at every moment
in her life to sound the currents
of opinion continuing to change
focus   what an eye untrusting
opens to time after time

she felt, she melded with
surroundance, one infers continuing
as an act of trust, until
the eye needs no more, and
the beauty says itself,
when focus is at last entrusted

to the movements a figure
constructs outward
an aural surround
to dance that space as if
a trust in every next step
instructs beauty's terrible reach

or beauty's most desirable mistakes
that sprawl new purity into
the space aural as figured
speech, practice of trust,
instructive in movement
as the outward ceases to yield fear

but yields to it / beauty's realm re
named as trust   lost to
dusty 'justice' / stories of
death dealt out for someone
s sake as 'the beauty of
the weapons' mis-takes again

apart from winter pear, these
winter temperatures turn elemental
weaponry with muscles flexed
to the point of an unyielding indifference
disguised as dedication, justice,
pressing forward into stories

frozen solid / the 'as if' of
narrative refused   an absolute
zero of muscled movement
all that lovely body
ing forth gone into the
world of righteousness

where mental cavities are filled
with absolutes, apart from
motion, replete with
refusal, stories are used
to lodge belief into
systems deemed infallible

and forgetting as systems will
how the long dull pain
panics thought away
pulls mind's muscles tight
against tales tallied hope
toward the starred sky   widening

to the place of thought,
long muscles leaving
a tight lane of scars
that would replace
considered pain pulled toward
a blessed amnesia

in such spaced time the telling
tells muscles to reach to
ward the metal machinations
holding back voicings
votaried vision vacated
their seedling throw outward

extensions of belief in senses,
modest trees with the capacity
to splay forward into reason
test machine's rote sustenance,
the thrown voice
textures former seedlings merely once

as evermore in hope they begin
to grow / might almost
seem to walk away
as the watching eye moves through
the greenlit underbrush
they came to on the wind

as things do, evolving,
watched or not, the 'splendent eye
loses focus as exterior beginning
to light underbrush as overgrown,
the wind is clear on green,
on sticks also, adjusting motion

as they wave or sway
branches reaching toward light
confuse the eye brought
slowly to an inward turn
while walking still as silent
breath sweeps wide across the veldt

smooth green expanse, yielding
in mind to walking toward
and toward, until a meditative
colour lifts thought into
a form of sleep that turns
branches to their roots again

xv.

the breath of disappearing
moments loses sunfall, folded
points filled with imagined
integers breeze toward
skin blessed with other
skin, through fields again

what is the point of aspiration,
is there a place to which dance finally
arrives, the step merely a metaphor
for something, perhaps a world within
the chosen calling that eventually confiscates
what inherently is there

taken away it goes further
than believed and the feet stumble
slowly to a stop beneath
the great blossoming chestnut tree
leaning toward seed reaching
out to the dancing stars

collaborating as the standstill snow
feeds earth its topmost layer
beneath which seeds won't stop
the breakthrough planned for
slow rising to stars from chestnuts,
their great shine

above the mirroring white glitter
gathering minds reach out
toward other worlds / other
words seed le blanc / cross
the gap / gate to wherever
blossoms dance the air

unmitigated freshness leaves
a twinge of glitter flexed across
the reach of words, these blossoms
from delinquent seeds mirror
the mind and dance and
gap up to being blessed

under the triumphs, scattershot
of looming clouds paced across
the glow of dance
guested in words of light
in mirrored sustenance, pure
boughs lifted, fallen into relaxation

a lazing of liturgy / letters
left behind beneath below
aglow they move almost stately
across the panorama shaped
by words lit up afar
a purity of discourse desire

prepared and yet relaxed into
the ritual of motion's pure
retracement of afar to mean
aglow, the words to this almost
a panoramic clarity
shaped like letters of selves

speaking / or inscribed into
a world moving always elsewhere
beneath the branches glowing
minute flares   far reaching
pinpoints filigree the night
traceries of entanglement

intending sparks a side of
thinking not thought beyond
yet / a rebirth flares
as desire opens toward
bodied world   whirled
about in dancing rhythms

remote as siftness once
removed singes the song
lost to third whirl tundra
various depths untangled from
and which and to the murk
intoned near basks of sky

spring shakes sprockets
free of function, popping
noise precedes the dark
conclusion, errant way
fare blokes its under-climb
toward opus, makeshift opulence

upon the thrum one
thinks around / around
the turns all carry forward
break and rise and tip as
dark is nigh the thought
is nigh the wellspring

whence all action shunts
across abyssal heights
or the ever darkening
green of waters forests
nights swimmers dreamt
beneath a toss of moonlight

washed so casually
against (encore) the brushed
young darkness pressed
against the height of act
green centre 'neath some
formal water

assume formalities as ways
between / trees statues
an assumption of mannerism
s sweet reach to peace
fulfilled in the musculature
reaching to a tidal pull

a magnetary pressure lures
impulse to acquiesce / equally trees
own musculature accorded status
of a tidal pull until
a wind draws reach
to form a form

upon place / torque / shadow
when in season shift
bestow torn before thin
foliage / a tide of prior
shimmerings glow forth
upon / against / and in

as wingspread warrior
stands / caught in
torque against
massing massive
blow / ballast
centuries' flotsam tossed

plyward as its purpose
shims a grasp at once
released from tautness as the
passing passive
show presses then
releases only moments

xvi.

tweaked by aura traced
above the lorn swath cut
sub tracting trees in hundreds
now away the many photographs
displace what once appeared
these possibilities

sweltering with/in in
finity yet — smaller filters
mold their transitive
entirety to lave the flings
into a modest prayer
for light and thinning

out / ward off
what may be mist
beneath darkened leaves
a casting out of reach
as if thread of focus
flutters flick new signs

plushward toward the seeping
equal to a whisper gift
even a stone, the lotus as
enclosed / mentation splends
its way as tones
once inside and now motioning

toward pure silence and stop
not a finish but a full slow
breath forever taking
in / seeming event
to ally with stone
its slow flowering

fractions of the day
relay the day from infra- ground
to uplane where the diggers
find a way to splice
the road / make patches
real more than the names

re-   placefully or tenaciously
in dented twice as flecked as
pace made shoulder to
shoulder length versus
chopped from carriage carried
in a way from in the way

stationed here there and
every air of vocal
culated belief / from lung
brought or bought up
as shares of / faux
humble being gone walkabout

gone white in wind
of cold calculation / how
measure honest breath / count
every taken toke in
broken promises propose
confusion / flickering in flames

tones blemish otherwise creamed white
expanse / a taken breath is
counted as the breakage slanted
with / in premises / a measured
calc / the talc of it in situ
breathing past confusion

clustered as we are all
in a state
these rights unequal to
these premises safe unsafe
(powder) safe unsafe safe
the snow becomes a job

to do or to be done by
buying out of
may being must tie
ideas to action
let 'us' go then 'you'
and eye the possibilities

action locates being / buying
in / the may swivels the icing
plocked right-gestured near
one norm or two the eye on
simplest rungs / the climbing
cursive as the counting

flies to sugar whitely
covering how the swivel
plonks a normative eyebeam
down / or through the rungs
belled bottoming out in
the crack where freedom wanes

lifting off in single file
through wear and torrid swift kicks
cover belly-up norms clothing
the apparent fire speckled
with bright beams some white
and some scattered

as intent leaps through
opposites   from water to fire
in air to ground an idea
thrown blind / the line
straggles between rocks
staggering up through fog

the drizzled lines versus
the cut lines / the dreamed lines
in a fog that lets go drams
idea owns intent through
staging / staggering / strands
part-way open up (the rocks, the blind)

led by themselves themselves
gone walkabout inside the radio
waves unisexual / no questions
from the distaff side / who says
nothing never / who says
how to reach right through the dream

gone to ground / or gravitas
of rubble rung to new tune
tone of battle   tons of bombs
explode any questioning
gaze beyond the mirror
stage for an action broadcast

laud fast tact where rage
is never yonder / where
a razing wrests the plosives
out of tombs the rattle
lunges in the place runes
remain the stubble that was town

gone down to darkness again
against the lauds and land
mines a trust broken
tact ticks off the wrong
implosive revenge factor
raptors rage above the torn ground

mounds of captors cage their prey
the lack of flow throngs
fraction after often
token blind brands
would hypothesize fraud
spoken toward wheat light

what eaten whey to go
beyond hunger to desire
but for what fortune's
nut bars no one from taking
blindly the tokened brandname
for predicted freedom or

xvii.

found dictum equally branded
sliced / factual largesse
attuned strenuous in termed
triage as hunger past
white noise shattering
least sum of colour / squared

the march into the square
defense denies any run
to round the corners off
into the slippery sidestreets
of rhetoric wrecked by
ways of barricade barred

collapsed the way primacy recency
appears   to have intended
roots of trees   notes
riffed blueblood   thought real
with/in the float of aspiration
quill as apparatus wrenched from

testament expresses thirds unsung,
the ground already broken
tithes of fallen thorns
as ruse still kept aside
is shorn   and few
dismantle woods as gloves fray

punctuation, the abrupt de
centred construct greening
thought grown in threes
trapped mythical from
a refraining boom
faux modular then flowing

entering the doorways of non
notation / rotation
ary note : ha / halved
in slewed slurred growl of
anticipation   : heard
as beauty grows into dark beginnings

twelve-tone / pentatonic / dia
tonic / dietetic few
appendages of beauty / all those
blanks that would not lighten
open as a door would / as expected
wood plays gravity against atmosphere

and rises toward what sheer
nest of chords swung from
here to here to there on
a farflung fifth draped
drippingly over a versus
voiced jagged and jogged by instinct

climbing wet and cold up
rocks cut against stars
where a lyric law lays down
the shattered head / dead
to the world at last   leaving
scrawled notes of pain behind

dissuasion comes after the long
wait / long look apart from
song and floating passages
purportedly torn from
what was whole / considered
such / with floating and with love

each quintessence spritzes
found smooth thrum of scatsung
f/light / bells rung by rung,
the mental shift comes down,
comes droned, as bells
by one round chisel dark

rocks clambered out and up
pitons there and pattycake
songs kid you knot
in hill / sideways hung to
dry run / desert
ed island sung through centuries

of swift and sweet and chisel
twice the nautical invasive
patent siderung split to
pieces this is
how we grow to island:
sung and hillways

carved / the blank eyes of
stone stare hillhigh down
to wavewander / wind
rung melodies hollow
ripples over fjord's
sungstruck moonwalkway

again again
st melodic plum to hollow
what wind otherwise
resounds in / of / with
tumult and the liturgy
of free walk spreely

spelunking notes call far
freedom rung through
hollows and hills beyond measure
meant to bring all fallen
saints home into clouds
winddriven and riven clean

echo masks first tone
or hills distend the fallen
clouds as wind drives
notes far from the free
home's streeted spectre
of all saints come clean

washed clean / the wind
swept curves of
curse of all fallen martyrs
claimed for and against and
wrongthought wrung barbed
wire and walls trumpeted too far

from boundaries as they are and
as they were claimed / wrung
for, forethought curved
swept rightened with-
in barbs of brass as
instruments / still instrumental

marching orders / odours of
race racing the news newly
minted / brass is as it acts
from behind the lost no(t)es
notched as a gun barrel
s song of death regardless

tracking the transplants
chanting lost things
that come in barrels / brass
tactics precurse nomenclature
racing past the odour and
the thought behind the thought

xviii.

practicing some thing
that can be summed / dis
tilled embargo wood sail
free traced then same-day
world freed of its saints
walking their baroque few twinges

twitched and twanged / the float
ing wood rings hymns of praise
as each doubled note
negates   takes
self away / waving
doubt down through green transparencies

the clean span of mown
laving / twelve shaken
(etched) sparks qualify
the rote pieced doubling each
raised tote bag's
spangled itch

backpacked and scratched for
or what twelve pastors
painted over cry to
an aching (arching)   sky
blue as any bent note
notched and carried outward

strands past paint re
verse the arching sigh,
the stray feel of lariats
in twelve smooth
backlit packs,
blue hewn tones

caught and hauled in
rid hard and rid of
never / the less said
sung or cried / as
the twig is / broken
space opens a silence for

blest sonne tools (the eye)
to lithe or snapped reed
opening to still (the less
said) spaced be
tween such urgent
rose and roses

warned and warring white
to red   (who chooses an
other colour / steps
out of the garden / the game
shows talk showed less
than spaced out sparks of light

sky / light of night
shades toward dark
framed as heart
swung to heat
seeking miss
ill winded

thinned as kilter
mean versus median
heart reveals heat's
seeking as the mist
tills harbours under
neath kismet in frame

do horses or kilts
dance there woven so
among the median branches
filling in behind canter
lake mist rising with
the blade in the hand

resistance dulled akin to
blades is made specifically
above the median,
where one projects
dance rising beside water
and beyond the horses

upsidedown bleeding
fallen above the wide staircase
staring upwards
the war continues hundreds
of years on / the dance
of swords light strikes down

blood dims the light
by hundreds / trance
impossibly becomes the upward
staircase / one falls
to one's age / swords
so specific / thin and small

but pistols expand (the reach of)
a ladder reaches toward heaven
on a building as large as the world
cannon signal final defense
final attack / how end
a war against idea / climb up

teachings would be laddered / if
and only if defense would
wither bravely into factual decision
point on point / ideas shifting
from attack to parallelogram's
unwitting construct

where no becomes un
knowing / instanted in
that hidden   nest
to rest there   unsure
patterns anathema   leaves
speech paranoiac / stone

cloned to feather
breast sans nurture
spare to hidden
taint / by spattering
non-random numbers painted
on required squares

computed the flight still
swerves / non
sense or random flick
of wind   winds down
stained (strained) hope   or any
move bishoped proleptically

as fate approaches, my bishop
moves before yours / winds down
sense, swerving at random /
straining to compute what in flight
is asked, appears
to have been blamed / still broken

and still crying in wilderness
swamp / all authorities
swooped change of direction
unchecked yet / yesterdays
continue toward a future past
blown there   papers strewn inform

whoever firsts the thing holds sway
though it is all forgotten
as strewn paper where a thing might have been
written chafed against apparent
surface yesterday thus equal
to today / predictive so the future (still)

carry on / carry what
load of first thought last
written catechism / how
lost the carved words of
how lost the heard words of
thunder said then but not now

xix.

only how solitary that figure
turned inward
eyes blank / a carved
and empty mouth winds
whirl through   / sculpted
mourning moaning meant

cold day carved by figure
dependent upon what other
eyes see / sculpting's only
history / an ill-defined version
of outward / blanking out
the inward truth in motion

this morning / looking in a spoon
he noted that concavity reversed
the image, while a convex view
was straightforward / pressing
code for the stretched spot
of momentum signaling within

that to see both ways
might almost be enough if
thought nested in the eyes
flight instead from
toward fight instead crumb
ling intelligence (lost in mist

too fine for this air
this art finished off
the paper torn and blown
screen cracked and dark
mirror of thought gone round
in circles never reaching out to

off-mirror, thought twins
circles around art's
unfinished miracle put finally
to paper, screened by darkness
and eventually reaching
the cracked surfaces

conserved the root sinks
beneath the green gone
of dried grass or dusk's
dominion / no light
flickers   waves or
particular menace named

moon maddened and made
manifest in turn and turn
again / against sparked
rhythm rising / timed
rite into foliage darker
against night sky falling

a drape tinged with hue
of foliage made rhythmic
in enfolding quiet lowered
as a rite against
the sparks of daylight
covered over turned away

till dusk expands the eye
or startling across the sky
a tree blossoms in exploding
light boom boom boom
percussive perception
s ritual forest brightening

lay them out on the table there
let who can come forth
let the stone be cast at
let the wassail bowl explode in light
let no one leave though
the forest green fills

a sketch   of this rage
planting allowance be
neath   breath's ex
plosive   final loss
where lakes grace charcoal
drawings grown to thrive

darkness blown off
dust of inscription
s anger augmented there
beyond lines drawn to ends
emotive and emanate   em
tied   into a brightning sky

etched against the surface
inscribed on darkness
anger chiselled to the ends
of brightness past
or infantile or dancing
tied to reflex tied to rising

wide and then blinked scansion
ripples across sight twinned
to light skimmed from such
dark pages / flipped as swoosh
of whitecaps blown tense
to drown inscription's twinkle

wrinkled script browns
in the lenses' prior white
whoosh chipped to darkness
limned from flight
thinned in the simple play
of poverty near mansions

wide to windsweep
blows blown facsimiles
thrown from room to room
an igneous confusion   contusion
of rainsteeped ideologies
ripped tidings new joy

confession at a time
like thing slows process nick
named progress configured as
a thriving ploy confined
to others' joy slipped
as a disk is roomy until closure

closed door's foreclosed
wept and waiting hoped for
giveness / a lean or
lien / the time counted
coined or counterfeit
fathered or feathered therein

with child one does not
close the door / one waits
so as not to mute
hope of the child / hope for
the child / if counterfeit
one protects as father / feathering

xx.

if father protects whose wings
shelter the child still beneath
or gone always as soon as
felt / that wary warrant for
spoken hope in the awed silence of
the garbage heaped awry

silken wings distill silence
beneath intended dissonance
replacing awe-forsaken heaps
of charity gone soon
before felt as the imagined
hope repairs protected places

light lost to time
s slippery sloped slough
wet wearing angles smooth
angels a glow of fiery
resistance / eons from
silver city emptied thought thins

silver's slight tone
pings from the instrument
with modest glow resisting
its own emptiness / a thinning
practiced time that angles
toward forthcoming fire

on the wind of sighs
signs across a page
ping at the fingers' ends
modest motion makes mend
the empty open space
now filled with burning tone

alone time tills the pace
of plenty tended modesties
the lingering near window
opening the hands
as lines on stage
the sighs

looking down toward
wash of sound
wish of sense modestly
withheld as harvest
of applause and in
taken breath released

brook's tincture
withheld from
camera released
of sound sense
harvested young
breath allowed

fogged lens
lets go
light lifted
above reflections
sensed inhalation
tint of moonlight caught rippling

absent the perceiver
slight prompts quiver
in the inhalation
of the ripples
embedded in the lens
the lift the lofting

felt seen and heard / or
missed / 'crossings in
mist' dream prompted
toward off / any inspiration
riding the rapids
through partitions construct

a cursive view of shaping
lopes across division
'spired through phases
rapidly formed in mist
a third of the seen
promptings ridden across

woods shapeshifted plain
views of white cursivity
cause casuisting as war
gaming gains precedence
cavalry formation founders
on mistwritten swamplands

cures taper war
along dreamed mist
preceding views of wood
that form shapes written over
lands preceding white as
depth as shift as game

played out / curses
crisscrossed the fading
wandering wood / rocks
blocked roots routed
while missiles 'rain'
rot through thought's negative

is there a feeling
of negation to match
thought resistance
what root goes where
all laws break down where
rain is played-out poison

and scofflaws reign
with poisonous precipitation
the only prep a ration
of non/sense made money
wise people foolish
acid lie of lost moonscape

violation spans the inner
globe to ration out
due worth contrary to
pantomiming the supposed tasks
of leaders as if sense
could be contagious

as if the senses gained
a kind of knowledge
felt on the tongue
a worn weave of
lies laid out
across diseased (dis)connections

when felt, things link,
including senses woven across
knowledge tongued
in triplicate as music
threaded with disease
or dissonance

that open mouth   that
scream of rage ragged
as the wings outspread
and beating almost broken
blowing ash   ripped cloth
words lost in flames

cloth bleeds remains
the wound ripped 'open'
vents against resistant
atmosphere absorbing
the inevitable ash
postscript of words in flame

xxi.

frozen in place again and
again seeing books burned
around the staked woman
written into after
words gleaming against dark
sky opening above stark eyes drowned

sky words written around
frozen openings that once
gleamed seeing on
above the after burn
a place a woman
eyes finally gone dark

shadowed pain there
's no there where ashed
waste / landed her
embered words / whipped
skyward on updrafts
captured unseen

whipstitch loosely gathers up
a form of sky as words
in draft the taken
shadow basted
on an image seeming
land with embers

burnt birds bade gone
flyabout desertscanned
heatwaves rising inter
ference / sightlined
sideswiped words
she stitched across clouds

a sure direction swerves
with force
s scans them without
thought of heat of foils
just takes the sky across
in and apart from clouds

gathering the lacy edges
in / sewn in thunder
around the head a
maze of lightning strikes
beyond rhetoric whispered
where cowled eyes hide

in sacrament or scorn
the whispers light
some faded headlines
gone to lace around
rhetorical maze
sewn to pieces

piecing to gather slashed
words piercing together
the slapped head / slagged
landscape of war
drummed as ritual
winds through charred corridors

what remains / drummed
lands at war
words / drummed
pieces winds press
through charred scapes
piercing

has priced peace beyond
warmusic / missiles
roar of bomb
winds winding through
emptied glassed canyons
corporate cantons (w)ashed clean

wound more than mere flesh
minds eyes wide silence
against glass wall
ed   negative beauty boot
falling across the mouth
muffled in earth dug deep

earth presses south
deep into negatives / mere sheet
of simple bathed in
chemicals / and look
at the glassy silent
moment there / apart from flesh

pushed and pulled as part
of the war pressured
deeper / loss of air
clean and breaths not held
against the yellow cloud
flash on the mirrored wall

war / simplest of responses
equals the mirror perfectly despised
prompts loss to quiet the equation
breath ceases cluttering
replaced by cloud's momentary
wall

rising ever higher above
thinking through clouds
stars still shine beyond
a light scattered mirror
mists miss while minds
righteously martyred blind

rinds of light
desist from minding
slight shattering
or scars that line
the loud blinks
of distant sifting

thoughts rising rind
driven / fixed
though   and stopped
fax flaming   green
screen exploding
seconds away

and on the threshold of
colourist finds there lives
a tiny flame / moments from rising
to unfastened flame
that drives the seconds
through the screams

xxii.

centre's many large rooms
emptied of coherence
the unheld   unhealed
wobble of dead
words   / worlds
apart hide from body's sense

some apartness worlds into
and via rooms
large and withheld from
centres as multiple
senses hide from
a cohering thread

threading through empty
corridors wisps of fog
ged thought a magic
talisman can't prevent
dissipation / dissent
unheard in the body politic

thought parts in
corridors that form a disparate
sentence immune to talisman
the would-be body magic plants
itself in fog where hearing
gels the thread ed facts

lackwit education fact
ors rhetoric higher than
intelligence   filtered
through corridored thinking
wound inward to hidden motive
conjured in the smoky pentagram

rhetorical indulgence takes up
space within the corridor
where motives ill-hidden
crowd out thought unequal to
the inward smoke of motives
feverishly dispatched to actuality

while actually withered rhetoric
seems to grow as smoke gathers
ever more dissipate / dis
pensate malignity's woven
mesh mashed against rot
spread / viral wordring

each clash dwindles to corrosive history
dispensing viral threads
unseen until there are no fibers
rich enough to reclaim a positive
rendition of the ping
elucidating former peaceful weave

history's woven page burns
outward a black growth
as fevered / unthinking
rhetors reach deeper into
martial music's magic meltdown
pangs ping on the broken string

plucking retributive stings
a felt-down musing
deepens reach to fling
toward growth most any
thinking and detach from
outward any vestige of a history

always written and now unread
always forget the sentence
laid out on staves stashed
away from / take away
the named music of time
deaf to what falls from the burning air

learning pairs with forgetting
tames the muse
removes contents of staves
in favour of contentment
each stashed sentence
waives the written from the read

given as gone / into the world
clouded as salted (Carthage
in flames   again and again)
written on the wind
instruments playing up a
storm troping against angst

shelter comes as figment
and again the wind
plays tutti insistently
as an instrumental urge
to self against the storm
requiring all the instruments

in tandem   song
lines scribed against figments
of imagination's lack
backed into corners
homemade twisted beams
tornadoed darkly toward silence

just before what strikes
comes an unearthly negative
of the strike itself
when something very like imagination
will unmake home twist line after
line into hideous song

silenced in the mist
gathering slowly and with
what gravity flowing
to cover all bodies in
shrouded knowledge they'll
'study war no more'

the quiet is itself
a study that transcends
the gathering in gravity
the flow the cover and the knowledge
paced and sure
the bodies ever moving

xxiii.

       move on   move out
       into a new blue opening
       of the air / sky above
       the mountains there cut
       by living water rush
       down to the fruiting earth below

       plumbago presses through fall
       blue flowers sturdy   small
       near eye light cymbal
       and taut hide continue
       toward dreams to come during
       the cleanse of hibernation

       rocky rivulets criss
       cross the cavern
       cast bluelit ripples
       of light upon the curving
       walls waiting snowfall
       sleep the long dream of spring

       thinning seasons gesture to
       the curves from here to stars
       concurrent with the blue in
       snow light just against
       the atmosphere above its
       long and present sleep

       under such tiny light
       shine snowglow
       mirror of spheres turning
       into lost histories of
       wars still running fire
       into each small home brokedown

the small is where each
ingredient of history is felt
the glow of tiny light
and snow repeating itself in fore
ground of war's resemblance to trickle-down
only with raging fire

as it enters a low doorway
with a swirl   a bow perhaps
the gentleman caller hitting
the high notes   burning
burning   come to the city
gone down to salt sown

how easy is the hearing
of these notes called low
how gone to gentle are the entry
ways / burned recollections
salting the storehouse of
door frames aswirl with city lives

even under fire   bomb
sites inverted into sub
marine crush   the city lives
its stunned folk will it
will step out from broken frames
into the burnt light of dawn

memory accumulates and then
disintegrates / a city
becomes the crush of all these
similar and dissimilar
ingredients that light
the stunning versions of the afterfire

in which the stunned survivors
stare alert and wonder
where the buildings went
the children almost play
in ash and broken plinths
scarred black and still falling

survival costs play / costs wonder
costs stones / forming
the numbness to endure
trades nerves in skin / the buildings
may be there though not
felt / scars erase the child in each

stoned moment survival
demands / a way
to clamber away
through rubble / skin
ned knees and arms hold
emptiness out as a gift

now thousands who were paid
earn what little from collecting
empty bottles / plastic things
that qualify / work hours
are the dark hours / people
on their tiptoes reaching into trash bins

scuttling down into craters
scattered with such televised
precision patterns across
a city once full of
the lived movement
moment matter made igneous

mere touch once
full of smoothness
and lived privately
scattered now into captured acts
turned moments spattered
into scavenging

caught sudden in savage
glare above   whirring blades
(blades!) hold perception aloft
targeting new possibilities
how sentimentality courses
bright colours across screens

coexistence (peaceful as a thought)
the softer dream minus
targets caught in blades /
back away from sentiment
bright posses limn then splay
the screens the streets in colour

almost black it runs anyway
in what once was home
blasted heath / broken
heather the flowers
bloom not further than
the suddenly bright green screen

home full of screens in layers
various / unbroken blooms
trace green vines across
the almost sudden showings
of the breeze and repertoire
of distances available

to see from / to know
as if from / such information
s a nation's call to arm
the man forget
ing all others sideswiped
by whose history's casualties

amnesia thought to be a gift
extinguishes first
the sides of stories
followed by the stories themselves
until a casual assemblage what was
seen ceases to be recognized

xxiv.

> given the giving told
> such stories pasttiming in
> to mostly assembled p
> recognition / causal
> boxes carry the eye
> into smaller smaller caves full
>
> as freedom of itself
> the string narration is when
> in the eye the smallest
> save is full as givens
> during crucial pastimes when
> in boxes all the carried things
>
> dissolve into the crannied
> possibilities / who'd climb
> into those caves if small enough
> but for the gleam and grain
> of each stepped image eyed
> and flung into the mirrored dark
>
> intoxicating fling toward
> even fictitious gleam with
> in stepped narrow r/eaches
> small and mirroring
> possible seeds to be
> come grain a hand can wave across
>
> dig in to what hoped for
> abyssal shadows filled
> with earth or its seed
> ed implications / each
> grained moment of ex
> pansion pression   polished

the sheen is underneath
the shadows and implicit
grain pressed from an under
surface seeds the polish
to be seen expressed
as hope in momentary place

paced slippery and fine
sands stone a rip
rap connection upwards
where long shadows fling
and scrabble at sheer sheened
blossoming summits sought

in the events themselves
creamed from plethora
then flung to places past
the shade the blossoms
toward sleek summits
hinged to being paced

tops floating on steam
ed pushup / clouds of
lost in   the shadows
cling and clamber with
each stem flowering
into darkness called

protect / called mist /
eventually water / shaded by
the clinging stems /
toward dark / clouds with
and with and into
pushed floating atop

such depths darker and
darker go / down
along lines laid forth
stemming tidal flow
wave links particles
a misted collage of ing

though gesture locates
what may rise the tidal
magnet and the mist toward
what requires no light
life finds its own
places broken before seaming

sewn or sown light
filled lines of
site / flight
fading into bright white
shadows wavelengths
seeded into distant punk

t sight revs generosity
these altogether butterflied
young shadows offer tiny
shade in yellow gray waves
lining seeds as distance
goes to lengths

each turn trammed
to fields shadowed
lined and written far
beyond sharply
grained radials
sighting toward occlusion

the blocked moments equal
grains sharply
felt and simply
shaded with fields expanding
them and written singularities
become the whole in turn

re turn and turn again
how that inscription
shifts the light ploughed
under such reflection
slid lid's shadow
covers the whole wide field

a few thin weeds versus
the plush shift toward
constant shine to lace across
unmasking what is present
as inscribed apart
from inferential turning

folded the soft page
plies implies a field
of yellow leaves
read and fallen (stars
angst against concrete
listed but unheard

is a fleck of quiet
just about a field beneath
the stars or is there folding
that resists the listed
leaving of the sur
faces implied

any resistance plied surface
faded in ambiguous circumstance
not with standing fast but
stood up   left for dead
lined scrolls of names
gone down gone far beyond

surfaces stand until
surfaces are lost as scrolls
named circumstantial gone and
possibly beyond the fade
of full resistance far
from lines with ambiguity

xxv.

     lined with ambiguity
     the face stands   still
     featured   still fractured
     not yet falling into
     the human   crowded brown
     ian motion   swirling below

     conceptual stone then stone
     a colour then some human formal
     fraction meant to be
     a whole immobile say-so
     ambiguous though featuring
     a fall not yet discerned a fall

     chipped wing ground rubble
     carved by bombs or
     bullets / yet blank
     marble eyes still stare up
     to strain toward some
     concept beyond beyond

     are there these real things
     wings seen where only
     stone is blank unto
     projected skies the eyes
     flat thus unstrained
     aside from chaos of untamed

     windswept and taking
     wing invisibly / noted
     notated melodies sweeten
     unheard shadowed intaglio
     inscriptions chain
     slippery chaos to stone

toned lapses in a ship
the chains rock / squeak
hear sweet harmonic
touch the lift
as sound first
felt is higher

wavelength push of
bow wharf clang
song enchant
meant to hold fast
against green gone
dark down to rocklock

place / tapped / open
once clanged / holds
long tone / green
dark / as wave
locks / push of bow
to long brush / slowing

each note strained
strangled chunkachunk
watered down / blue
and falling / rolling
into gone wave
length of ship's sway

the pipes give way
the length / the ship
rolls over and across
the water and the watered down
strands of lean notes
in a single wave come clean

the gaze(d) upon
the night sky opening out
as starbelted figures
step carefully across
rivers of phosphorescence
sway beneath black branches

lines trace branches / slight
across night sky /
river their way above
each figure carefully as plans
move to tunes
of wind / form steps

dancing then her way
through lengthening skeins
of light strewn out to
ward the dark draped lonely
out between the whirling
galaxies of song

plain see-through song
consists of notes strewn over
what is rumoured to be darkness
lengthening the state of dance
between tall obligations
drawing shadows from the trees

all these pure waves
intermittently break open
until vision takes
the form of static
still remote as distant
language shining

a glow worms through
black holes undis
covered coursed
fragments filing out
from clouds of static
whirling into larger brightness

perspective altogether
in the fibrous layers yields
full view including black w/holes
filled with thought
grown whirling into
prior fragments forming cover

music of the smallest spheres
each hinged to each small
empty open
ing impressed   imploded
language breaks / or
breaks out a sudden brightness

happens by itself no one
pressed to breakage
force yields sudden
fazing of the traces
left as atoms
of the language

scattered remnants
blown far go down
into tunneled darkness
where sun momently
drops its light s(t)inging
on letters carved in stone

tones and fetters chart
these tines of f/light
as moments stun
the lark within the field
whose stark tune
shows as fractions

counted / counter
tenored notes rising as
the sun   the other birds
heard far beyond those
opening fields   fracturing
splayed shadow groves

no birds this morning
fields and wooded places
tended without rising
beyond open shadows fractured
by counter groves
perceived far from the sun

Douglas Barbour and Sheila Murphy have been actively engaged in the creation of *Continuations* since November, 2000, and its emergence has come to represent a part of both writers' daily practice, woven integrally into their lives. The work encompasses two nations within the North American continent, and reflects the experience, perceptions, and challenges associated with Edmonton, Alberta and Phoenix, Arizona. Both writers are engaged in their communities, and the long poem encompasses points of intersection that characterize diverse perspectives and discoveries that come together in a single work. Composing alternating six-line passages on a nearly daily basis brings with it great reward. This format inherently possesses flexibility that facilitates a fluent interchange, and allows a blending of resources associated with diverse backgrounds and experience.

Sheila Murphy's interest in collaboration was crystallized in response to *Absence Sensorium*, a book-length collaboration by Tom Mandel and Daniel Davidson, published by Potes and Poets Press in 1997, based upon its exemplifying a sustained, collaborative endeavour in which the book was jointly composed and credited. George Lakoff called the volume "a great long poem that is seamless." Despite occasional, prior appearances of collaborative writing, this opus appeared to signal the advent of a new era in poetry.

Absence Sensorium would precede Lyn Hejinian and Leslie Scalapino's *Sight* (Edge Books), by two years. In the latter work, authorial distinction was used, allowing the reader to experience separate passages as individual contributions to the larger work. Other more recent works of superb poetic collaboration in the United States include *Literature Nation* and *pleasureTEXTpossession*, both by mIEKAL aND and Maria Damon. These enormously significant works break out of the usual distinctions associated with literature and engage at a very rich and deep level, incorporating available technology and engaging in "interwriting," which opens the connectivity in the act of creating.

In Canada, Douglas Barbour and Stephen Scobie have performed extensively in sound poetry, in the innovative tradition of The Four Horsemen, Rafael Barreto-Rivera, Paul Dutton, Steve McCaffery, and bpNichol. Other sound poetry groups, such as Owen Sound, also 'wrote' performance pieces in a collaborative manner. Further innovative and accomplished collaboration by Canadian writers includes the work of the group Pain Not Bread, formed in 1990 by Roo Borson, Kim Maltman, and Andy Patton. Anne Szumigalski and Terrence Heath's *Journey/Journée* (rdc press), like Hejinian and Scalapino's *Sight*, clearly indicates who wrote what. *Double Negative* by Daphne Marlatt and Betsy Warland specifically works to merge the two writers, with a poem, followed by a self-interview, and then a series of pieces written out of lines in the earlier poem.

United States poet John M. Bennett has composed and performed joint works with numerous other writers, many of whose texts have appeared in the long-running magazine of textual and visual poetry, *Lost and Found Times*. Sheila Murphy has worked extensively in making collaborative texts with Bennett, as well as Peter Ganick, mIEKAL aND, Charles Alexander, David Baratier, Ivan Arguelles, Rupert Loydell, Lewis LaCook, Al Ackerman, and Beverly Carver, among others, including a collaborative quartet with Mary Rising Higgins, Gene Frumkin, and John Tritica.

Countless examples of poetic collaboration are evident on the web, including works initiated on listserv groups, such as the *poetics* list from the State University of New York at Buffalo, in which poets representing many different countries have participated over the years. Many collaborative works exist across artistic disciplines, rather than within the textual realm: Robert Creeley collaborated extensively with visual artists such as Jim Dine, Alex Katz, and Susan Rothenberg, as well as composers such as Steve Lacey and Steve Swallow; Lyn Hejinian has collaborated widely with artists such as Emilie Clark, with the appearance of *The Traveler and the Hill and the Hill*. Numerous others have collaborated across disciplines.

In contrast to the aforementioned long works, a great number of collaborative efforts are of short duration and characterized by brief experimental formats that depend upon novelty. Methods such as *exquisite corpse*, deriving from the surrealist tradition, often serve to reveal unconscious linkages that accompany structured collaborative exercises.

Students of innovative textual work will undoubtedly pose questions concerning the place of collaborative poetry: *What is the relationship between collaborative efforts and the individual works of a writer? Should collaborative texts be regarded as a category of their own, or classified within the sphere of innovative textual creation?*

We share the belief that textual collaboration must undergo the same critical rigour as any written work of literature. The process of jointly writing an extended piece naturally entails risk, but the sustained engagement with crafting what is possible in language easily surpasses such risk. Stabilizing structural features such as the six-line format and daily practice, provide the necessary structure for propelling innovation.